Christmas Wreath

Make your own Christmas wreath using both twigs and origami.

(Nuts)

①  ②  ③  ④

Upside down.

Finished

Follow steps
① to ⑪ on page 4 of Vol. 2.
Upside down.
Fold the remaining three parts.

Do the same
on the other side.

Pull to shape it.

Basic Rules

Fold in the reverse
--- direction of the dotted
line. This is known as
the 'mountain' fold.

Fold along the dotted line
--- in the direction of the
arrow. This is called the
'valley' fold.

— Cut

(Wreath at Right)

Prepare two fairly
thick tapes of
different colors.

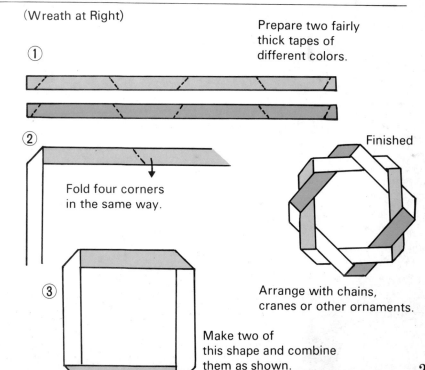

Fold four corners
in the same way.

Make two of
this shape and combine
them as shown.

Finished

Arrange with chains,
cranes or other ornaments.

2

3

Christmas Wreaths

It's easy to make all these out of paper.

(Balloon)

①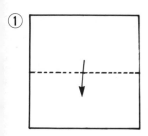

②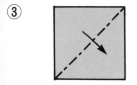

③

④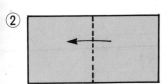

⑤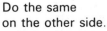
Do the same
on the other side.

⑥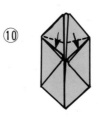

⑦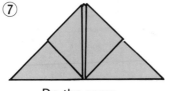
Do the same
on the other side.

⑧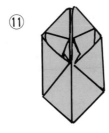

⑨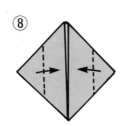
Fold the other side
in the same way.

⑩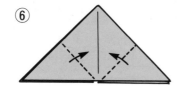

⑪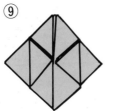
Slide each head
into pockets and blow up
the folded balloon
through a hole.

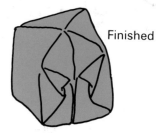 Finished

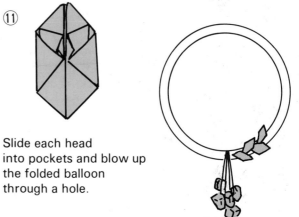

Paste the leaf (please refer to page 11 of Vol. 2) in thick paper.
Cut a circle out of thick paper, and paste leaves on it.
On how to make other wreath, please refer to page 2.

(Wreath of Tape)
Finished

① Prepare a long tape.

② Fold A and B
alternately.

③ Paste to fasten
at desired length.
Add wire on the back
to shape it.

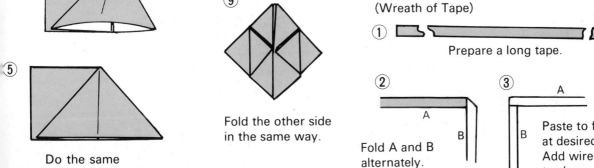

4

Candle Holders

You can handcraft beautiful candle holders with any paper at hand.

①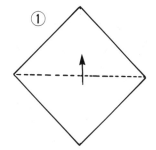

②

③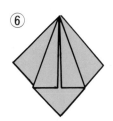

④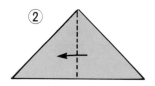

Do the same
on the opposite side.

⑤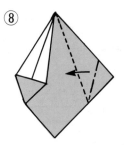

⑥

Do the same
on the other side.

⑦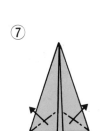

Fold so as to open
up the inside.

⑧

⑨

Do the same
on the other side.

⑩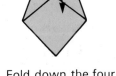

Fold down the four sides
in each direction.

⑪

Make the inside
round to form the box.

Finished

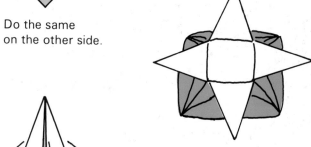

Use one color over
another for a more
beautiful effect.

6

See page 13.

Horses

All of the animals rejoice in the birth of Jesus.

①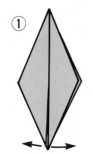

Follow steps
① to ⑫ on page 6 of Vol.1.

②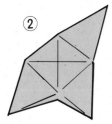

Turn it over.

③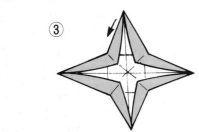

④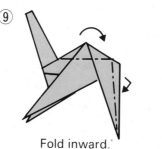

Fold both sides
in the same way.

⑤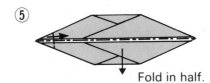

Fold in half.

⑥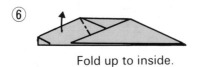

Fold up to inside.

⑦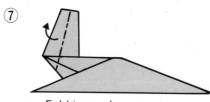

Fold inward.

⑧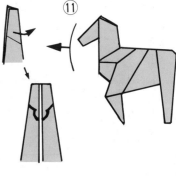

Cut

⑨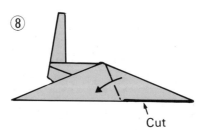

Fold inward.

⑩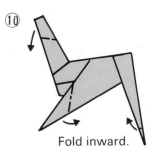

Fold inward.

⑪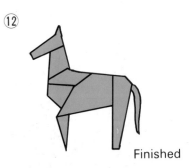

Open and cut the inside.

⑫

Finished

Pull out again
and fold.
Add the tail.

Three Wise Men

They came guided by a star, bearing precious gifts.

(Three Wise Men) Use paper with white back.

①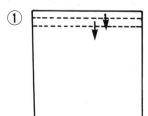

②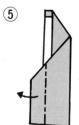

③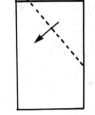

④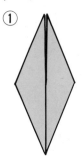

Do the same
on the other side.

⑤

Finished

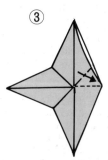

(Star)

①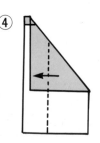

Follow steps
① to ⑫ on page 6 of Vol. 1.

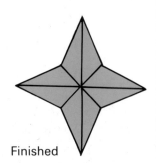

Finished

②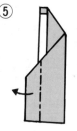

Fold one sheet
up in back.

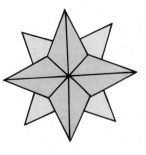

Make 2 of these
and paste them
back to back, as shown.

③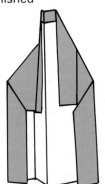

Fold up and open.

12

Nativity Set

Baby Jesus in the manger, Mary, the Three Wise Men and animals recollect the glorious tale.

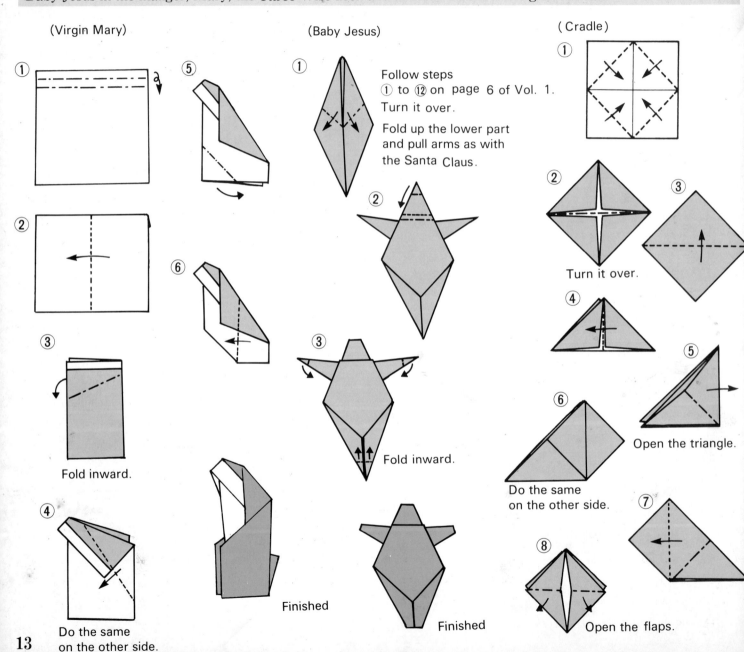

(Virgin Mary)

① ② ③ Fold inward. ④ Do the same on the other side. ⑤ ⑥

Finished

(Baby Jesus)

① Follow steps ① to ⑫ on page 6 of Vol. 1. Turn it over.

Fold up the lower part and pull arms as with the Santa Claus.

② ③ Fold inward.

Finished

(Cradle)

① ② Turn it over. ③ ④ ⑤ Open the triangle. ⑥ Do the same on the other side. ⑦ ⑧ Open the flaps.